# THE SHELL BOOK OF MOTORING HUMOUR

# The Shell Book of Motoring Humour

Introduced and edited by
NICOLAS BENTLEY

MICHAEL JOSEPH
LONDON

First published in Great Britain by
Michael Joseph Limited
52 Bedford Square, London, WC1B 3EF
1976

ISBN 0 7181 1520 1

This book was designed and produced by
George Rainbird Limited
36 Park Street, London W1Y 4DE
in collaboration with
Shell U.K. Limited

Designer: Trevor Vincent
Printed and bound in Great Britain
by Jarrold & Sons Limited, Norwich

# Contents

# Introduction

# INTRODUCTION

It is a powerful tribute to the resilience of human nature that, after all that the motor car has done to mankind, we can still look upon it not merely with a tolerant eye but often with amusement. It is just as well that we should be able to do so, because whether we like it or not, it looks as though the motor car is here to stay – at least until some more ingenious or economical method of transport is invented to take its place. And if that seems to give a facetious emphasis to what must surely be self-evident, you have only to look at cartoons such as those of Alken, Cruikshank, Robbia and others to realize that some sort of alternative to the car may one day be born from a union between, say, the thermo-nuclear engineer and the industrial designer who specializes in high-velocity stresses.

Those who in their superior wisdom smiled at the mechanical fantasies of Alken and Cruikshank are hardly to be blamed for failing to foresee that, within a comparatively short time, some of those fantasies would be translated into realities, sometimes not very far removed from what those artists had envisaged. Yet such an idea would have seemed as remote in 1830 as the possibility would have seemed in 1930 that within forty years men would be taking trips to the moon and, like terrestrial trippers, would depart from it leaving behind unsightly evidences of their visits.

The first appearance of the motor car produced, except among the minute body of its enthusiasts, a reaction typical of the public when faced with something new or strange: people were either hostile to it or sceptically amused by it. And it is interesting that although we have since come to accept as part of the natural order of things a vast intrusion of the motor car into private and public life, there has not been much modification of either of these attitudes. The car is still often an object of abuse or derision.

But it would be stupid as well as ungenerous to the memory of those who invented their various versions of the motor car not to give it its share of praise as well as blame. If in some ways it has diminished the quality of life by making man its slave rather than allowing him to become its master, in many other ways the car has made life a lot easier and more enjoyable than it was when journeys by road took longer, were often more hazardous, and a great deal more inconvenient. But more than that, the car often has an ennobling effect on our characters. Think of the patience that a motorist needs when he or she is stuck in a traffic block; think of the reserves of fortitude they must have to cope with a breakdown on a lonely road, or the

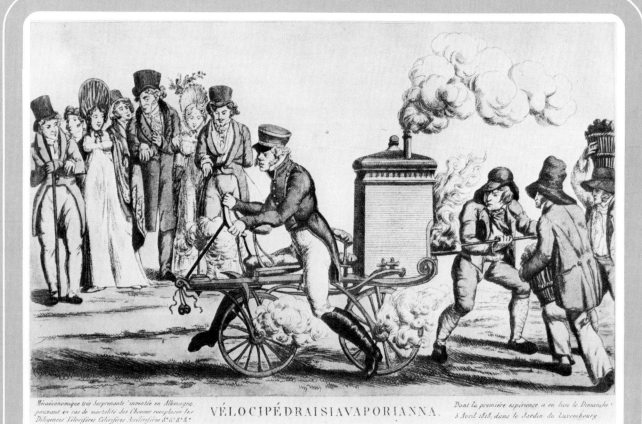

Véloséconomique très Surprenante inventée en Allemagne; poussant en cas de mortalité des Chevaux remplacer les Diligences Vélocifères Célérifères Accelérifères &c. &c. &c.

VÉLOCIPÉDRAISIAVAPORIANNA.

Dont la première espérience a eu lieu le Dimanche 5 Avril 1818, dans le Jardin du Luxembourg.

ingenuity that must be exercised to find a safe spot in which to park in almost any metropolis; not to mention the tact you need to try and pacify a beady-eyed warden. These are attributes unlikely ever to be as fully developed by the man who has only a bicycle or his two feet to depend on. And he is a good deal less likely than the motorist to see the funny side of motoring. You need to have had first-hand experience of the sort of problems and dilemmas with which the motorist may be faced in order to appreciate their effects; their effects on others, that is, for by the definition of that shrewd and neglected philosopher, Will Rogers, everything is funny as long as it happens to somebody else.

Only the motorist, therefore, can really appreciate the possibilities of humour inherent in the mere fact of someone else being a motorist. To start with, there is the

The Amazing Mechonomic! Invented in Germany this machine could, if horses were to become extinct, replace coaches as well as *Vélocifères*, *Célérifères*, *Accélérifères* [early forms of the bicycle]. The first trial took place on Sunday, 5 April 1818 in the Jardin du Luxembourg.

laughable fiction that man is master of the machine, his own creation. The machine knows better. It has only to strip a gear, ingest a piece of grit, spring a leak or burn a valve to reduce the driver's proud mobility to static impotence until the matter is put right. And not all motorists are so mechanically minded as to be able to put things right themselves. Some are too impatient, some cack-handed; others are timid about what they may find under the bonnet; and there are those who are unaware even of how to open it. For each situation of this sort there is always a humorist ready to exploit it.

9

Human relationships, often a source of amusement in themselves, seem almost as fruitful in the context of motoring as they are in the domestic or political spheres. Drivers (especially those who occupy the back seat), passengers, pedestrians, policemen, wardens, magistrates, garage mechanics, petrol-pump attendants, road-menders, and of course other drivers, are all potential subjects for hilarity. So are stray dogs, traffic regulations, road signs and mechanical defects. In fact, few other fields or activity or experience can provide so many possibilities of raising a laugh.

The earliest recognition of these possibilities came with the earliest concepts of the motor car, as we see in some of those nineteenth-century cartoons which visualize a variety of ludicrous futures for mechanical transport. Even before the turn of the century, *Punch* began to publish jokes about motoring. In 1898 the famous figure of the Michelin Man, a deliberately comic approach to a vital aspect of motoring, made his first appearance. Not long afterwards Harry Tate's music-hall sketches, 'Motoring' and 'Selling a Car', had his audiences rolling in the aisles, and comic

In 1825, in Yorkshire, George Stephenson launched his *Rocket*, which flashed from Stockton to Darlington, a distance of some eight miles, at the frightening speed of 12 miles an hour. Inspired by this glimpse of the possibilities of mechanical transport, visionary crackpots all over the place began to devise and to experiment with a variety of steam-propelled horseless carriages, with results that gave cartoonists a golden opportunity for fun at the expense of scientific enterprise.

*Above* A View of Regent's Park, 1831; a prophecy of the progress of steam, by Henry Alken, published in 1828.

*Right* Another 'Modern Prophecy' by Alken: Novelty of the Year, 1829. The caption forecasts a situation dismally familiar to the modern motorist: 'I say, Fellow, give my Buggy a charge of coke, your charcoal is so dear.'

songs and postcards about motoring were
as popular as those about drunks,
landladies, and bathing belles.

Not all of these early motoring jokes were
as feeble or as ingenuous as most of them
seem nowadays. On the contrary, some were
quite ferocious, some even sinister. We are
inclined to think of black comedy chiefly as a
theatrical phenomenon, a type of grim
humour which, to begin with, appealed only
to limited audiences in out-of-the-way
theatres. Samuel Beckett, Jean Genet, and
later on Joe Orton, were among the chief
prophets of what was at first regarded as
this new and questionable cult. But was it
really new? And is it any longer
questionable?

As early as 1903 artists in newspapers and
magazines were already making jokes about
bloodshed, mutilation and even death
caused by road accidents. Though most of
them were fairly crude in concept and
execution, jokes of this sort are direct
antecedents of black comedy as we know it
today: a style of comedy based on ideas and
situations in which those involved are so
outrageously lacking in ordinary feelings of
revulsion, pity or distress that they belong
to a realm of their own from which have been
cast out any vestiges of sympathy or of what
is implied by obsolescent ideals of 'good
taste'. So huge is the gap between the
horrific humour of this strange and rather
alarming world and the sometimes painful
realities of our own that we laugh at such
jokes through sheer incredulity, as we do
when we see ourselves in a distorting mirror
or drawn by a caricaturist.

Like most other people of the pre-Victorian era, the artist George Cruikshank viewed the possibilities of the steam carriage with a certain amount of scepticism.

*1st horse :* A Coach without Horses! ! ! ! nonsense – come, come, Master Dobbin, you are 'Trotting' but you must not think to hum [hoax] me because I'm blind!
*2nd horse :* Well, dash my Wig, if that isn't the rummest go I ever saw! ! !

*1st dog :* I say, Wagtail, what do you think of this new invention?
*2nd dog :* Why, I think we shall have meat cheap enough! !

In three-quarters of a century motoring as a source of humour has become in the Western world almost as prolific as drink or incompatibility between the sexes. But will our descendants find the subject as amusing as it has seemed to us since the advent of the motor car? Looking at the pictures in this book and reading what has been written in a light-hearted spirit about motoring, it would seem that opportunities for making fun about the internal-combustion engine and its vast penumbra of mechanical, legal and social consequences are limitless. From the earliest jokes of Meunier in *Le Rire*, Caran d'Ache in his *Lundis* and Raven Hill in *Punch*, through the ingenious imbecilities of Heath Robinson to the glorified chariots of Steinberg in the *New Yorker*, there runs a vein of comic invention that suggests that those who may look for further possibilities will continue to find them somewhere, somehow. The theme of locomotion is virtually ageless and that of the car has become universal. What are Steinberg's chariots of chrome and cellulose but an echo of the chariots of Nahum the Elkoshite, who more than six hundred years before Christ forecast a scene that has become a commonplace in our own time.

*The chariots shall rage in the streets,*
*they shall justle one another in the broad ways :*
*they shall seem like torches,*
*they shall run like the lightnings.*

    Nahum, 2:4

Long before road casualties became a matter for public concern there were those who refused to regard the motor car as anything but a menace, though this did not inhibit the humorous artists of the day.

*Above* An illustration by W. Ralston from a cheerful motoring story of 1896.

*Left* A hypothetical contretemps at the Automobile Club's show at Richmond in 1899, as envisaged by Ralph Cleaver.

ILLUSTRATED ADVERTISEMENTS
YOU START THE MACHINE
THE MOTOR DOES THE REST!!!

I hope to run across you soon.

The publishers of comic postcards have always been quick to exploit the most recent of society's preoccupations. Motoring was an obvious choice of subject, even as early as 1904, when these light-hearted examples appeared.

Motorist - "Hello, killed anything?"
Sportsman - "No, have you?"

# The Early Years

## THE EARLY YEARS

Between 1900 and 1910, give or take a year or so, little change occurred, so far as the ordinary pedestrian public could tell, in the design or appearance of the motor car; it remained essentially a primitive-looking vehicle, though most of those who owned cars no doubt considered them to be completely up to date. Nevertheless, by comparison even with the models of the next decade, the earlier cars were slow, cumbersome and erratic. There was also an air of novelty about them and as in Britain novelty is often regarded at first with wry scepticism, or else with facetiousness, the motor car became an immediate butt for humorists.

That a good many of their jokes now seem pretty feeble is hardly surprising. Fashions in humour are liable to change as quickly and as decisively as fashions in women's hats or shoes; those that were regarded as the quintessence of chic in 1900 have now become items of period costume. And the jokes of that period, which, like its hats and shoes, now seem just as antiquated, also retain an intrinsic interest as examples of the popular taste in humour.

As pioneers of motoring, the French were no less keen or enterprising than the English, as is shown by the selection of drawings that follows, these being taken from both French and English sources. The French, with their reputation *pour l'amour* and their traditional interest in fashion, tend perhaps to emphasize the sentimental and sartorial side of motoring, while the British, also true to form, show a stronger preoccupation with the mechanical side of things.

AN EXCELLENT INVENTION

With motor-cabs, a substitute for 'Whip behind!' becomes a necessity. Messrs Start and Jumpkins's patent galvanic urchin tickler will be found most effective.

To achieve picture postcard status was a sure sign of public recognition. This series of cards (*c.* 1900) shows that the vogue for motoring was steadily increasing. Here the car is an important feature of what seems to be a sad little story of unrequited love.

THE HONEYMOONERS

*He :* 'Heloise! . . .'
*She :* 'Gaston! . . .'

*Opposite* Robida's *New Vehicles with Various Engines*
1. The grocer delivers his goods to your door.
2. Carriage for nurse and baby.
3. 'Herrings, frozen herrings!'
4. The pastrycook's boy delivers a *bombe glacée*.
5. The milkman's vehicle runs on the steam that heats his milk.
6. The luggage porter.
7. The policeman uses an electric car to control traffic.
8. The woman who delivers the bread.
9. Motor-tricycle for the landscape artist.
10. This mobile dwelling will take you and your belongings anywhere you like, whether moving house or going on holiday.

*Right* Among the first to appreciate
the comic potentialities of motoring
was the French cartoonist Caran d'Ache.
Here in 'Chauffeur et Contre-Chauffeur'
he takes the careless motorist to task.

### ADVICE ON MOTORING DRESS

The only way to enjoy a motor-car ride
through a dusty country:
adopt costumes of the above type,
hermetically sealed and warranted dust proof.

### LOVE AT THE WHEEL

*He :* 'My throttle is wide open for you.'
*She :* 'Careful, my friend, you'll damage your magneto.'

Woman motorist's padded foundation garment . . .
and some coats for angular and rotund
women travellers, and those in love.

The Michelin Man, one of the most famous and perhaps the most long-lived figure in the history of advertising, made his first appearance in April 1898. Since then, in innumerable guises and situations he has continued to delight the motoring public.

Robida's *Modes du Jour* for motorists, male and female.
1. '*Violette*' – light, misty and delicately veiling a charming face.
2. The 'Thug' – a head-dress derived from the Indian stranglers. Not to be worn too tightly.
3. The 'Diver' – should 15 metres of rain fall, one can laugh; indeed, with this head-piece one could salvage the galleons of Vigo.
4. The 'Calabrian Brigand' – elegant and strictly incognito.
5. The 'Capote' – would almost do as a mask for the carnival at Nice.
6. The 'Sea-lion', the 'Seal' and the 'She-bear' – practical costumes that allow their wearers to brave all weathers and even the most icy blast.
7. The 'Chauffeur's Umbrella' – would make a delightful opera cloak.
8. The 'Orang-outang's Hood'.
9. The 'Helmet' – a thirteenth-century heaume is reborn.
10. The height of fashion in the old traditions of aristocratic elegance.
11. *Robert le Diable* – 'You nuns who rest under this cold earth. . . .'
12. The '18th Century' – enables the wearer to go hunting.
13. The 'Road-hog' – 'Look out, there's a dog on your nearside and a pedestrian on your offside!'
14. The 'Wolf' – 'What big eyes you have, Grandma!'
15. Protection against the winds – simple and convenient.
16. The 'Speedy One' – the retroussé nose caused by driving at speeds of 46 mph and over.
17. Overcoats in rhinoceros hide, proof against rain, hail, mud, tempest and almost against cannons.

A THOUGHTFUL MAN

Mr Jenkins drove his new motor car down to Epsom; but, to make sure of arriving there, he thought it only wise to
bring his horses as well, in case anything 'went wrong with the works'.

*Opposite*
Caran d'Ache offers
his impressions
(on the public)
of a road race from
Paris to Bordeaux.

SAINT-CLOUD Go!

VERSAILLES (7 km) 'Get out of it, you pig!'

CHARTRES (79 km) 'What in God's name – !'

CHÂTEAUDUN (124 km) 'Scallywag! . . .
Lout! . . . Wretch! . . .'

VENDÔME (163 km) 'Damned son of a bitch!'

TOURS (220 km) 'God's mercy! . . .'

CHÂTELLERAULT (289 km) 'Parisian thug! . . .
Murderer! . . .'

POITIERS (321 km) 'Devil! . . .
Anarchist! . . .'

ANGOULÊME (431 km) 'My cow!'

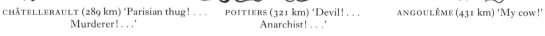

556th km Ecstasy!

557th km Bordeaux at last!

The level of early motoring humour was not very high, but this example by the artist Tom Browne probably reflects fairly truthfully the type of facetiousness that early motorists had to put up with.

*Opposite*
Robida's imaginary designs
for motoring gear were in some cases
not far removed from the real thing,
as is shown in this drawing
by Sabattier, not intended as a joke.

# A Day on the Ripley Road

Nowadays there does not seem much to be said for this sort of elaborate joke with its feeble denouement. But no doubt the motorist of 1904 would have appreciated it, as long as he was not the victim.

*Right* I drive cautiously and am determined to consider other people.

*Below* So, when passing a nervous farmer's wife, I render profuse assistance amidst profuse thanks from her spouse.

*Below right* I am passed by a brother motorist, who yells, 'Measured distance ahead!' Query: What does he mean?

More mystery. Sailing along an empty road I perceive a white flag waved in the distance.

Suddenly I am stopped by a policeman, and am confronted by an affable detective with a stop-watch.

I am summoned
for furious driving!
*Mag.* (loq.): 'What have you to say?'
*I*: 'I was only go–.'
*Mag.*: 'Pay three pounds.'

Injustice drives me to
seek safety for the future
by adopting other tactics.

## INCONVENIENCE

*I collided with some 'trippers'*
*In my swift De Dion Bouton :*
*Squashed them out as flat as kippers,*
*Left them* aussi mort que mouton.
*What a nuisance 'trippers' are !*
*I must now repaint the car.*

Harry Graham: *Most Ruthless Rhymes*

WHY SIDE-SLIP?

Our artist offers his three Patents gratis to the World.

From the beginning of the motoring era until the car assumed its place as a factor of major importance in our social and economic life, jokes about speed seem to have predominated over all others. Certainly, although accidents involving injuries were fewer than, for instance, breakdowns, speed and the risks that it incurred were the favourite subject of the humorous artist.

*Racing driver*: 'It's not the bends I'm bothered about, it's the straight lines in between.'

BROTHERS IN ADVERSITY

*Farmer*: 'Pull up, you fool! The mare's bolting!'
*Motorist*: 'So's the car!'

Breakdowns, if not as popular as speed, were still a constant subject for humour. The jokes about them, some of which now seem innocent enough to make one wonder why they should ever have raised a smile, did at least reflect a constant preoccupation not only of the motorists but of their passengers as well.

THE JOYS OF MOTORING

No, this is not a dreadful accident.
He is simply tightening a nut or something,
and she is hoping he won't be much longer.

*Opposite* Even before the First World War, another problem – one that was eventually to become a matter of anxiety not only for motorists but for the public at large – had cropped up and soon began to restrict the motorist's mobility. This was the traffic jam, for which, in 1914, *Punch* suggested some solutions.

The Run-under Cycle-car; goes *anywhere*.

The Concertina Car. For use in tight places.

The 'Lift-up' Side Car.

The Expanding Cow-Pusher. Will shove off anything.

*The Surrey Policeman*: 'It's no use your hidin', Sir, I must 'ave yer name and address.'

# Interregnum: 1914-1939

## INTERREGNUM 1914–1939

In its earliest days the motor car was generally regarded as not much more than a plaything for the mechanically-minded plutocrat. However, just before the First World War the cycle car appeared; having more in common with the motor cycle than the car, it was an attempt to provide low-cost transport for the masses and it flourished into the 1920s. After the war the car took on a new status; it came gradually within reach of the merely well-to-do; it replaced the horse on a wide scale and came to be looked upon more in the light of a necessity, though still by no means indispensable. Meanwhile Henry Ford had put a stop to all that. If Ford had been less ignorant and less narrow-minded he might have been ranked as a genius. As it is, his place in history – which, with the complacency of the hardened philistine he derided as 'bunk' – is no more than that of the first high priest of mass production in the motor industry. It was by him that the first step was taken in the process of sanctifying the motor car and in next to no time he had elevated it to the status of a household god. But even after this the car was still considered to be a legitimate subject for joking; a change from the sacrosanct attitude enjoined upon the faithful of most other religions.

An artist who delighted in sending up motorists and the motor car was H. M. Bateman, a disciple of Caran d'Ache, yet at the same time a humorist of true originality. Bateman's name has become synonymous with the type of awkward or embarrassing situation in which his victims usually found themselves. Among his best-known cartoons are those that showed the lighter side of the First World War.

The stowaway

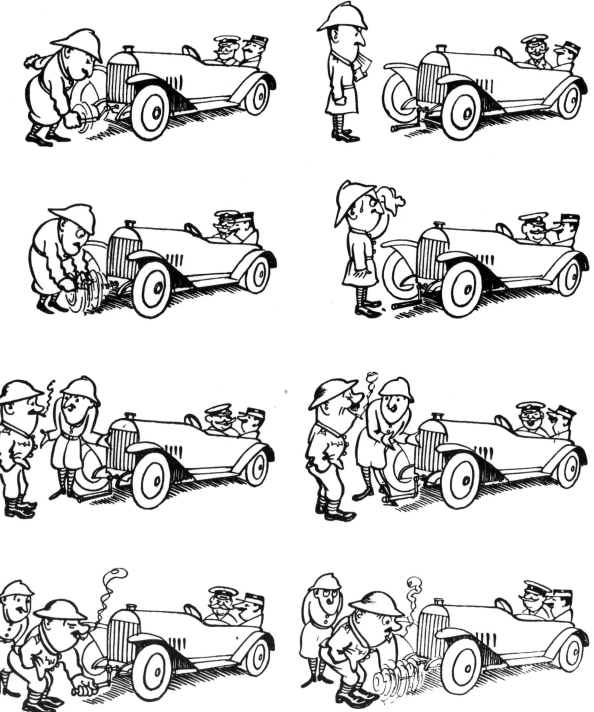

The Optimist

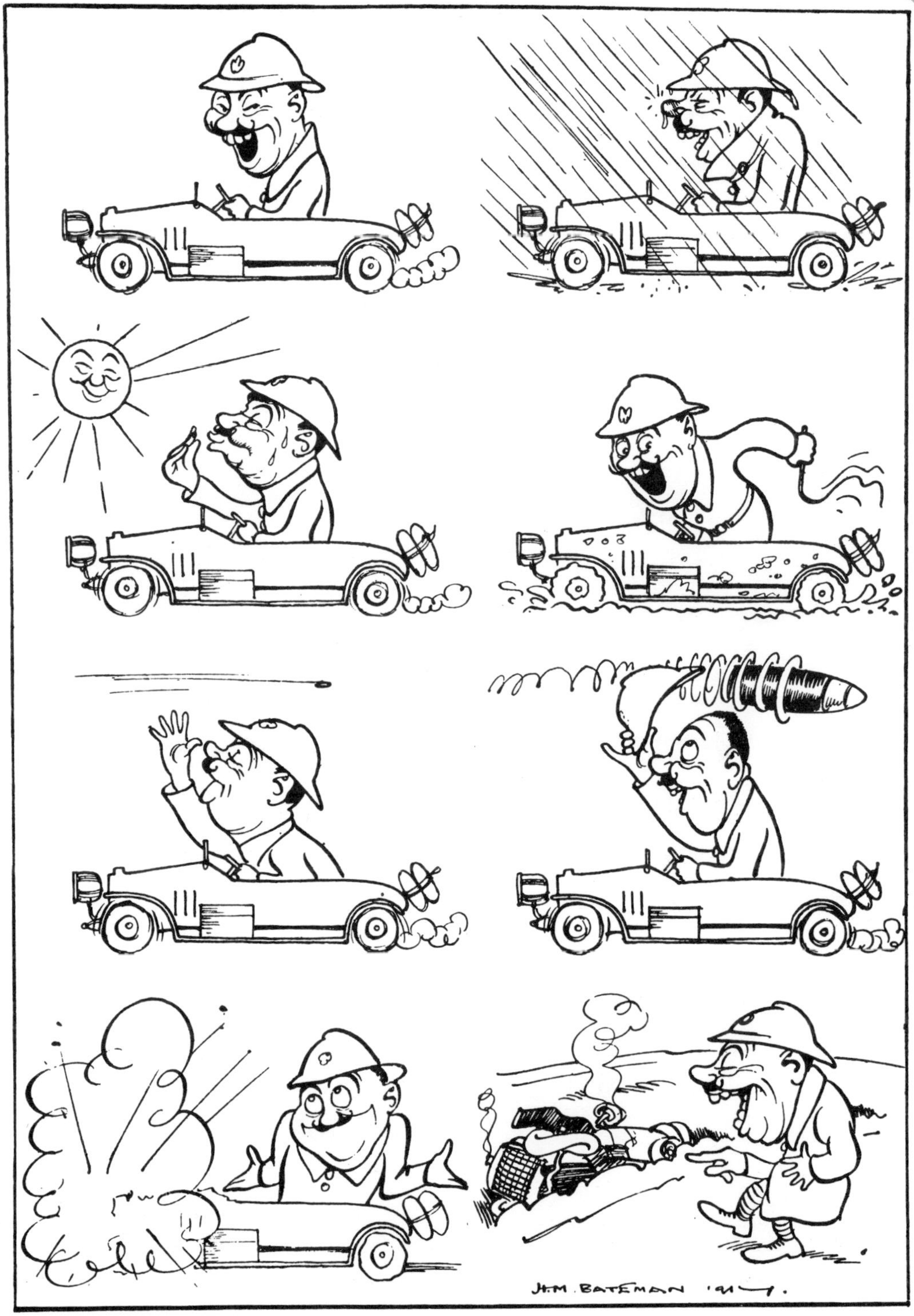

ONE OF THOSE UNFORTUNATE CASES—

--IN WHICH THE SUPPLY IS BY NO MEANS EQUAL TO—

—THE DEMAND.

# Lead, kindly light

Motoring in the 1920s was often full of surprises and a day's outing was consequently more of an adventure than it is likely to be nowadays. Maurice Wiggin, who, as a small boy, lived at Bloxwich in Staffordshire, remembers very well the hazards of a journey of ninety-odd miles in an overloaded Tin Lizzie when, for their holidays, he and his family made their annual pilgrimage to Rhyl in North Wales.

No sooner had we all got loaded up than 'Sam! Sam! I can't find my bag!' cried our mother. Everybody knew that all the money was in mother's bag. So dad, who was just climbing up into the Ford, climbed down again with a prayerful expression on his face and went back into the house to have a look. I got down from where I had been sitting on Uncle Tom's lap in the front and began to play about underneath the dashboard, turning the brass petrol tap on and off and enjoying the smell of petrol and brass and American cloth and wood. Then dad came out into the yard looking harassed and said,

'Our mother, I've searched high and low and it beats *me* where you've put it. Are you *sure* you haven't got it in the car with you?'

Everybody in the back of the car began to rustle and squirm. That was, our big girl and our little girl and our cousin Bert and our mother and Aunt Fanny. Bert and our little girl were sitting on biscuit tins full of food and there were about seven or eight bags and boxes stacked around them, mostly full of food, but some of them holding buckets and spades and bathing costumes and one with the kettle. Cousin Bert trapped our little girl's finger between two boxes and she began to holler, though she was a brave little girl. So she was passed over the heads of the crowd to our dad, and he kissed her finger to make it better. Cousin Bert had his ears boxed by Uncle Tom, leaning over from the front seat, and our mother said, 'Oh, Tom, don't hit the lad. He didn't mean to hurt her.' And Uncle Tom replied, 'Pardon me, Lucy, but I know better.'

Climbing up from underneath the dashboard I banged my head on the ignition lever and before I could stop myself I said *bugger*. Our big girl heard me, if nobody else did.

'Our mother!' she yelled. 'Our mother! Did you hear what he said? Our mother, did you hear? . . .'

I looked round to put my tongue out at her and caught Cousin Bert's eye. He was smiling. I winked at him. He winked back and then he turned to our mother and said,

'Auntie, *I* heard what he said. He said *bugger*.'

There was a terrible commotion then, everybody yelling and trying to get at everybody else. Before I

knew what was happening Uncle Tom put me down off his knee and opened the door and climbed out. He rushed round to the back door and hauled Cousin Bert out and he put one foot on the running board and started to tan Bert's bottom. The running board fell off and Bert rolled under the car and Uncle Tom bumped his head on the side. Our mother began to laugh and everybody else laughed, too, as they always did when our mother began to laugh. Then we all got out of the car again and stood around looking at the running board and the grown-ups were wiping their eyes. Bert quietly crawled out on the other side of the Ford and began to run away up the Sandbank. 'That boy's got the devil in him this morning', said Uncle Tom, and he began to run after him.

'Well,' said our dad, 'we can't put *this* lot right in five minutes. Mother, you might just as well put the kettle on . . .'

We had a cup of tea and some bread and cheese and pickled cabbage and Uncle Tom and our dad came in from mending the running board and had a wash . . .

Bert and our little girl and I went out and bagged our places in the Ford. The others came out and climbed in and our dad began to swing the starting handle. The engine started, but as soon as he had climbed into his place and put his cap on back-to-front it died away. He got out again and swung the handle until he was blue in the face, and then Uncle Tom got out and swung until *he* was blue in the face.

'That's funny,' said our dad when he could speak. 'It was all right first thing this morning.'

He put his cap round the right way and began to test the ignition with a screwdriver while Uncle Tom swung the starting handle. There was a sizzling spark at every plug.

'It must be the juice,' said our dad. He got out the tool roll and unscrewed the petrol pipe at the carburettor. There was no petrol in it.

Our dad walked round and put his head under the dashboard and turned on the petrol tap.

'That there tap was turned off,' he said. 'You didn't happen to touch it with your foot, did you, Tom?'

'I might have,' said Uncle Tom. 'I'm very sorry if I did, though, Sam. I wouldn't have had it happen for worlds.'

'Oh, *Tom*!' said Aunt Fanny.

'Never mind, Tom,' said our dad. 'Least said, soonest mended. Now if you're all ready, perhaps we can get on. This rate, we shan't be in Rhyl before midnight.'

'Dad, dad!' said our big girl. '*He* was down there, where that tap was turned off. He was playing down there ever such a long time. Perhaps he turned the tap off, dad. And our dad, when he got up he said *ever* such a horrid word.'

'I don't want to hear any more about it,' said our dad. He pulled the ignition lever down its quadrant and the note of the engine changed. It began to pant eagerly. Our dad turned his cap round back-to-front and pulled it farther down on his head.

'Let's hear no more about it,' he said. 'Now have you all done? . . .'

Dad put his foot down on the pedal of the epicyclic gear and let off the handbrake. He pressed the pedal down into low gear and the old Tin Lizzie began to shudder and groan and it moved forward very slowly towards the road, puffing out smoke. We turned left out of our yard into Bell Lane and slowly gathered speed.

'Ta-ta, Bloxwich!' our mother cried in a singing voice.

'Ta-ta, Bloxwich,' we all screamed. 'Ta-ta, Bloxwich . . .'

Through Wyrley we sang 'Lead, Kindly Light' and through Landywood we sang 'Jesu, Lover of My Soul' and through Bridgetown we sang 'Keep the Home Fires Burning'. On we rushed, quivering and singing, and Uncle Tom got out his bag of chocolate shapes moulded in the form of flat animals as Gailey came in sight.

'That's the first ten miles, then, Tom,' our dad shouted triumphantly above the wind and the sighing of the car.

Uncle Tom eased me away and pulled his watch out of his waistcoat pocket. 'Barely three parts of an hour, Sam,' he said, and our dad nodded in a satisfied way and answered, 'It makes you wonder what they'll think of next.' 'Yes,' said Uncle Tom, shaking his head, 'it's wonderful.'

Ford
THE UNIVERSAL CAR

SELLING AGENTS EVERYWHERE.

£135 COMPLETE.
AT WORKS: MANCHESTER.

"ALL THE WORLD LOVES A — FORD
— EVEN THE MOON BEAMS —"

'That's a puncture,' our dad said as the car began to bump and hobble along. 'Well, I declare.'

He stopped the car and turned round to address the back seat. 'Now don't all start creating,' he said firmly. 'It's only a puncture. Tom and me'll have it right in a jiffy. You might as well get out and stretch your legs . . .'

We had another puncture before we reached Ivetsy Bank and a third just after we had forked right for Newport at Weston-under-Lizard . . . Then we had five sooted plugs in succession and the fourth puncture didn't come until we were almost on the outskirts of Whitchurch . . .

We had five more punctures between Whitchurch and Chester and our dad had to stop to buy a new box of rubber patches. He and Uncle Tom didn't bother any more to put their coats back on after a stop. They drove along in their shirtsleeves and we went so slowly and the day was so still there wasn't even enough wind to make their shirtsleeves billow. We had stopped singing and after the sixth puncture everybody in the back refused to get out even though our dad warned them that the jack would probably collapse under their weight . . .

'There's one thing, Sam, I've had a bit of practice now,' said Uncle Tom, unrolling the tool kit. 'A few more trips like this and I should begin to know my way round these here machines.'

'Oh, well, now, Tom,' our dad said, 'this is exceptional. Very exceptional. I mean to say, you expect a few punctures and sooted plugs on a trip this length. But *this* many . . . Oh well, there's no rest for the wicked, I reckon.'

'We must count our blessings,' said Uncle Tom, pumping away at the handle of the jack. 'I'd sooner be here than down the pit, anyway, Sam.'

Our dad did not reply at once. He was working the rubber solution into a smooth lake round the hole in the inner tube. He . . . pressed the patch on to the puncture, and Uncle Tom grated a bit of french chalk on to it. 'You're getting a dab hand at it, Tom,' said dad, smoothing the chalk round with his thumb . . .

Dad and Uncle Tom were heaving the tyre on to the rim. They stiffened, or at least dad did, and a tyre lever flew out and caught Uncle Tom on the knee-cap. He hissed with pain, but our dad never noticed . . .

Everybody was happy and refreshed now and full of a spirit of adventure. Uncle Tom and dad whipped on the wheel and we chugged up the big hill in bottom gear with clouds of smoke pouring out behind and everybody singing 'Rocked in the Cradle of the Deep', and as we did the last mile or two to take Rhyl by surprise from inland the sun dropped below the rim of the world and the western sea was on fire. 'Look at the sunset,' said our big girl, and we all looked at the sunset, driving into it at eighteen miles an hour, rising and falling on the metalled road, burnt and dusty and brave.

Maurice Wiggin: *In Spite of the Price of Hay*

## LORD GORBALS

*Once, as old Lord Gorbals motored*
*Round his moors near John o' Groats,*
*He collided with a goatherd*
*And a herd of forty goats.*
*By the time his car got through*
*They were all defunct but two.*

*Roughly he addressed the goatherd:*
*'Dash my whiskers and my corns!*
*Can't you teach your goats, you dotard,*
*That they ought to sound their horns?*
*Look, my A.A. badge is bent!*
*I've a mind to raise your rent!'*

Harry Graham: *Most Ruthless Rhymes*

The Michelin Man,
still with us
in the 1970s,
has appeared in
many different guises.
Here are some of
those he affected
in the 1920s.

The inestimable benefits that Women's Lib has showered upon the frailer sex can hardly be said, even by the most fanatical liberator, to have included an improvement in the standard of women's driving. That began to improve many years ago and it would be a rash man, as well as a prejudiced one who might try to maintain that now there is any difference between the reliability of men and women as motorists. At one time, however, before women had acquired as much experience of driving as men, there was perhaps some justification for regarding them as a mild menace on the roads, and since innumerable jokes were made about this, it seems appropriate that one should be included.

## BALLADE OF A SECOND-HAND CAR

*It is not long since I was sold*
  *A car by one who then did swear*
*That it was worth its weight in gold –*
  *A vehicle beyond compare;*
  *Since then my hours of peace are rare,*
*I ask: 'O Death, where is thy sting?'*
  *I've plumbed the hollows of despair –*
*Why did I buy the bloody thing?*

*I feel unnerved, infirm and old;*
  *The plugs burn out, the tyres lose air,*
*The carburettor catches cold*
  *And answers not my anguished prayer;*
  *And miles and miles from anywhere*
*My petrol needs replenishing,*
  *I find I lack some vital 'spare',*
*Why did I buy the bloody thing?*

*The starting handle, I was told*
  *Would start her when, from batteries' wear*
*Or chill, she had to be cajoled:*
  *This simple faith I cannot share;*
  *I tried. It caught me unaware,*
*And now my arm is in a sling,*
  *My backbone is no longer there –*
*Why did I buy the bloody thing?*

Envoi
*(to the insurance company)*

  *Dear Sirs, (You wonder how I dare?)*
*Herewith my claim for damaged wing:*
  *That makes the forty-fifth repair,*
*Why did I buy the bloody thing?*

H. S. Mackintosh: *Ballades and Other Verse*

Heath Robinson's name has become a by-word for eccentric mechanisms, to the principles of which he applied a kind of lunatic logic. They could never have worked, but how often has one wished that they might have done so, for invariably they were designed to solve some vexing problem for which no other solution existed. The shaky, makeshift contraptions which he devised in such detail, and the equally shaky, makeshift characters who manipulate them, exist in a solemn and polite world of their own. The urbanity of its motorists, for instance, never deserts them, even in the most hazardous situations. What an example to the rest of us!

On the following pages are shown some typically ingenious schemes – the Rescue; an illustration to *Omar Khayyám*; A New Adjustment for Motor Buses to Enable Pedestrians to Cross the Road during a Traffic Block; and finally The Ghost, a macabre motoring drama.

"A Loaf of Bread, a Jug of Wine and Thou,
Beside me singing in the Wilderness.
Oh! Wilderness were Paradise enow!"

*Rubaiyát of Omar Khayyam.*

A NEW ADJUSTMENT FOR MOTOR BUSSES
RECENTLY ADOPTED, BY THE L·C·C TO EN—
ABLE PEDESTRIANS TO CROSS THE ROAD DURING
A BLOCK IN THE TRAFFIC

W HEATH
ROBINSON

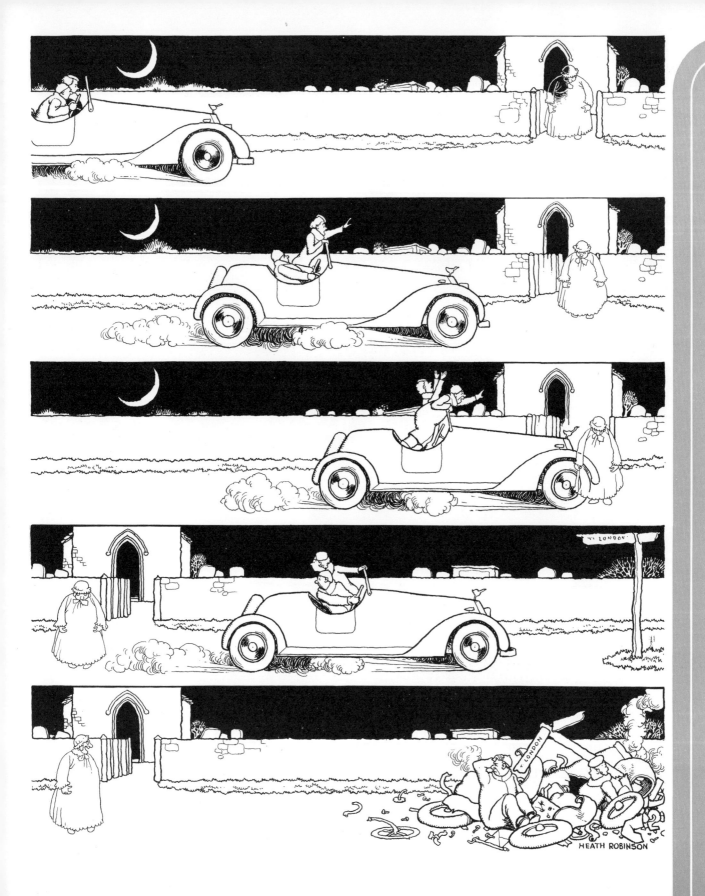

HEATH ROBINSON

# Max on Motoring

Sir Max Beerbohm was no lover of the motor car, though he admitted that in the early days of motoring he found a certain exhilaration in travelling fast. But Max was the epitome of leisureliness and therefore the enemy of all those processes of acceleration by which we delude ourselves into thinking that because the pace of life is faster than it used to be life must therefore have become more agreeable. Max did not share this point of view: nor did he see the modern motor car as necessarily an improvement on some of those earlier models.

Cars were not the things they are now. You didn't have to creep into them and crouch *in* them and squirm *out of* them. They were wide-open to the elements, and wind-screens were unknown. And in fine dry weather, as you sped along the roads at what seemed then a terrific pace, the air rushed into your lungs with the utmost violence, making a new man of you – and a better man of you. So as not to be blinded with dust, you wore large goggles over your eyes. But dust entered into your ears and nostrils and into the very pores of your skin. And all the while you were moving not forward merely. The machine was such that you were continuously bobbing up and down, and oscillating from side to side. Your body was taking an immense amount of wholesome exercise. Insomuch that when the ride was over, and you had gone and vigorously shampooed the dust away from you, you felt that you were now an even newer and a still better man . . .

In a sense, mankind has always loved speed. Speed here and there, speed in season, has always been acknowledged to be great fun. The Marathon race was a very popular institution. So were the Roman chariot races. One is probably right in supposing that Adam and Eve used often to race each other round the Garden of Eden, very blithely. Dick Turpin's exploit on Black Bess would have commended itself in any era to the people of any nation. So would even the involuntary adventure of John Gilpin. Dear to us all is the thought of Puck putting a girdle round the earth in forty minutes . . .

Roads are a painful subject nowadays . . . they are places for motorists only. And the motorists themselves are not comfortable on them.

The other day a motoristic friend of mine was complaining to me bitterly, even violently, about the behaviour of pedestrians. They were abominably careless and stupid, he insisted. I hate to see anyone agitated by a grievance, and I tried to soothe my friend by an appeal to reason. I said, 'No doubt we pedestrians are very trying. But you must remember that, after all, we were on the roads for many centuries before you came along in your splendid car . . .'

We are constantly told by the Press that we must be 'traffic conscious'. But there is really no need to tell us we must be so. How could we be otherwise? How not be concussion-apprehensive, annihilation-evasive, and similar compound words? . . .

The main root of the mischief is that great fetish of ours, Speed.

I have friends who argue brilliantly, and in perfect sincerity, that Speed in itself is no danger. They say that if the traffic were slower than it is the number of accidents would be increased. And they quote figures, and draw diagrams, and are as able as they are technical; and I am very much bewildered. If a man said to me, 'Oh, well, England is very much over-populated . . .' I should understand his point of view, though I should not share it. Nor do I dispute the proposition that Speed in itself is no danger. A cannon-ball fired from a cannon is not in itself dangerous. It is dangerous only if you happen to be in the way of it . . .

But here is a heartening fact for you. We are all of us travelling at a tremendous rate, and we shall always continue to do so . . . Our planet is not truly progressing, of course: it is back at its starting point every year. But it never for an instant pauses in its passage through space. Nor will it do so even when, some billions of years hence, it shall have become too cold for us human beings to exist upon its surface. It will still be proceeding at its present pace: *1,100 miles a minute.*

Sir Max Beerbohm: *Mainly on the Air*

## TRAGEDY

*That morning, when my wife eloped*
*With James, our chauffeur, how I moped!*
*What tragedies in life there are!*
*I'm dashed if I can start my car!*

Harry Graham: *Most Ruthless Rhymes*

# You have been warned

The first publication of the Highway Code by the Ministry of Transport in 1941 was not greeted with any great display of public enthusiasm. That was reserved for an unofficial manual dealing, though in a somewhat different form, with much the same subjects as are covered by the Highway Code. It was called *You Have Been Warned*; the author was Donald McCullough, the illustrator Fougasse, and the success of the book was immediate and enormous. No doubt this was partly due to the fact that its appearance and language were a good deal nearer the understanding of the average motorist than the stilted professional prose of the MOT experts by whom the Highway Code was compiled. Some passages in the McCullough–Fougasse version of the Code are no longer relevant; rules and regulations have changed, so have driving techniques, but much remains that is still worth consideration, as the following extracts from this invaluable work will show.

CORRESPONDENCE COLUMN

*My darling Angela,*

*My dear, guess what has happened. Daddy has actually promised to give me a car, and I am so excited I can hardly spell. Anyway, what I want to know is – as you know all about them will you please advise me about choosing one. I think I ought to have a fairly small one, preferably grey with red leather seats, because of that dress I got the other day, but I'll be guided entirely by you, as you're the only person in the world I can really trust and everyone says you have to be awfully careful when buying a car. Above all I want a good gear. A girl near here has what she calls a sports car, and she says the trouble with it is you have to keep on changing the gears. Do you think you could be an angel and tell me of some kind of car that has got one really good gear that will go on for about a year without having to be changed? I think that would be simply perfect.*

---

### 𝔉amous 𝔏ast 𝔚ords

'Which is the throttle?'

---

*I have only once tried to drive and I feel rather strongly that a car with some sort of bumper would be best ; as you know, the people round here are very old-fashioned. I suppose you heard that Henry never married that girl after all. Mrs T. was perfectly speechless with fury for months, but I must say that we all laughed like a row of buckets.*

*Another thing is going backwards. Our garage has only got one door at present, so I suppose I had better have a car that can go both ways ; I believe they nearly all do.*

*I know the Doctor's goes back quite marvellously. His small boy drove it last night right into the orchard. You simply must come and stay with us next month, the fruit is simply marvellous, and Mummy has got three first prizes for marrows – or rather, a marrow.*

*The only other thing is miles per gallon. Daddy says this is frightfully important so perhaps we had better have some.*

*I must stop now,*

> *With love,*
> *Prudence*

P.S.

*It must be small, because the roads here are so narrow and full of buses, and it must hold four people because of the dogs and parcels and things.*

*Dearest Prudence,*

*I know exactly the very car you want – it is a 20-litre two-seater sports Tornado. It has just about enough power for what you want, and as for reliability, it has done over 100,000 miles since it was overhauled in 1922. Its present colour is primrose and it has its name, 'The Yellow Streak', painted on the side, but you could have it re-done any colour you like, and of course a hood could easily be fixed on somewhere.*

*You would simply love it, I know, and the price to you, darling, will be very reasonable indeed. I will drive it over tomorrow if I can, but it may be the next day as it's been in our garage for some time now and may want something done before it will start. I'm so thrilled to think that you're really going to have it.*

*All my love*       *Your Angela.*

ROADHOGMANAY

. . . of course most of the trouble on the roads would be avoided if people would only cultivate a sense of proportion and stop driving much too fast in the hopes of saving five minutes that they don't know what to do with when they've saved them and then they would be able to drive a perfectly beautiful machine along a perfectly wonderful road in perfect peace and toleration as I'm doing now instead of thinking they've got to roar about and hoot and risk everyone's lives by cutting in like the fellow in the blue car in front which only makes them get into a filthy state of nerves over anything likely to hinder their foul progress like that madman who's just passed and if they only realized it they'd get there just as quickly and easily if they took it perfectly calmly as I'm doing now or anyhow they would if only the ridiculous way they go on didn't hinder everyone else like this blithering idiot who's just turned right across us and if half-baked louts like this man just in front didn't glue themselves to the crown of the road and make one hoot at them till one's completely deaf and if half-witted pedestrians like that one didn't simply hurl themselves under the wheels whenever one appeared suddenly round a bend and if this type of lorry-driving fiend didn't lumber about the roads hiding everything in front so that one has just got to trust blindly to luck every time one cuts in front of them on a corner and if absolute raving lunatics like this one didn't hurtle at full speed along a main road quite oblivious of the fact that we might be dashing suddenly out of a side road at the same moment and if everything else on the road didn't take a perfectly hellish delight in getting in one's way and making one lose precious minutes and blast you will you get out of my – CRASH TWANG TINKLE BUMP. . .!

CONCLUSION

'The average motorist', said my companion, 'is a much-maligned person. Contrary to the general belief, he does *not* go about the country intentionally courting disaster: he is as much concerned to avoid accident as any one else. Nor has he any desire whatever to jeopardize his own safety or his neighbour's. Being essentially law-abiding, if he is told by authority what he ought to do, the average motorist will always . . .'

At that moment a car came swiftly and suddenly out of a concealed turning, backwards and on fire.

'Why, bless my soul,' said my companion, 'there he is!'

Fougasse and McCullough: *You Have Been Warned*

---

### Famous Last Words

'It's all right, she's not in gear.'

'Run me over if you DARE!'

'Run me over if you like.'

**Famous Last Words**

'Quick, that's our turning.'

'Sorry, but I'm a stranger here.'

WHAT IT FEELS LIKE WHEN YOU MAKE A REALLY BAD GEAR-CHANGE

Arthur
Watts
25

Frank Reynolds was art editor of *Punch* in the days when good draughtsmanship was a tradition of which the British Press was proud. Though he enjoyed himself most when he was portraying the common man, the common motor car was also one of his favourite subjects. This drawing and those on the following pages show him combining both interests.

Our nature correspondent writes to us that the countryside is looking almost perfect.

A TRAGEDY OF CONGESTION

**THE HANDY LITTLE CAR.**

# Poeta ex Machina

Few poets of any consequence have written about the motor car. An exception is Sir John Betjeman. With his acute and idiosyncratic perception of significant detail he mentions a variety of cars – Hupmobile, Delage, Rolls-Royce, Bugatti Sports, Morris 8 and 10, Hillman Minx – the names of which arouse instant memories of period or place in those who share his nostalgia for the same dead days or remember similar occasions. Though not, as some seem to think, primarily a humorous poet, Sir John sometimes conveys by the unexpected use of unconventional imagery a humorous effect, as in his autobiographical poem *Summoned By Bells*:

*Here on the southern slope of Highgate Hill*
*Red squirrels leap the hornbeams. Here I see*
*Twigs and serrated leaves against the sky.*
*Once a Delaunay-Belville crawling up*
*West Hill in bottom gear made such a noise*
*As drew me from my dream-world out to watch*
*That early motor-car attempt the steep.*

Sir John Betjeman: *Summoned by Bells*

Again in a poem called *Exeter*:

*The doctor jumps in his Morris car –*
    *The surgery door goes bang,*
*Clash and whirr down Colleton Crescent,*
    *Other cars all go hang;*
*My little bus is enough for us –*
*Till a tram car bell went clang.*

*They brought him in by the big front door*
    *And a smiling corpse was he . . .*

Sir John Betjeman: *Continual Dew*

This shows that the motor car, though not in itself a very poetic subject, may be made to seem so when it is touched by the antennae of a true poet.

SING HEY FOR THE OPEN ROAD

Britain has a high tradition of satire and among its satirical artists David Low is one of the greatest. Though cars seldom featured in his drawings, those that he included were drawn with the accuracy and economy that characterized all his work. Forty years ago, when this drawing appeared, it was still possible to regard the traffic jam as something of a joke.

## PROGRESS AT PELVIS BAY

Sir Osbert Lancaster has long been known as a pungent and authoritative critic of the urban scene. Nothing, not even the Blitz on our major cities nor the planning blight that has since settled on a good many of them, has had a more marked effect on their appearance than the continuous increase in road traffic. Although forty years have passed since the first appearance of his book *Progress at Pelvis Bay*, much that Sir Osbert had to say then about the effects of the increasing ubiquity of the motor car on the traditions and amenities of a small urban community still hold good. Among those effects was notably the appearance of that inferior substitute for the coaching inn, the roadhouse. The pseudo-baronial type of establishment that Sir Osbert described is not often to be seen nowadays; instead there is the motel, usually less pretentious and more appropriate to its purpose than the fanciful conceptions of the twenties and thirties.

But let us begin with the transport of Pelvis Bay.

It was thought that the following pictures of the various types of public conveyance that have at different times operated in the vicinity of Pelvis Bay, drawn from contemporary sources, might possibly be of some interest to the modern reader . . .

The first shows the old-fashioned waggonette or char-à-banc that used to run in the summer between Pelvis Bay and various beauty-spots in the neighbourhood . . .

Next comes the first motor vehicle (a two-cylinder, chain-driven De Dion-Panhard) ever to ply for hire in Pelvis Bay. It was put on the road by the enterprising Mr Smith in the summer of 1908 and made several successful trips along the coast until it finally

exploded on the hill going up to Pelvis Magna one hot afternoon in the summer of 1909 – a laughable incident that was fortunately attended by small loss of life and caused considerable pleasure to several of the more old-fashioned residents.

Thus Pelvis Bay, ever progressive, can justly claim to be the scene of the first serious char-à-banc disaster that ever occurred in this country!

It is a far cry from that ill-fated machine to this typical specimen of the splendid modern fleet of motor buses and char-à-bancs that offer such

roadhouse, but few, we suspect, are acquainted with the history of the old place.

It seems probable that a farm-house of some description had existed on this site for several hundred years . . . The oldest portion of the present structure, however, goes back no further than the late eighteenth century.

In those far-off days there was little or no traffic, the road indeed being little better than a winding cart-track . . . but towards the end of the last century with the invention and speedy popularization of the bicycle there was a change . . .

The Widow Bloodworthy, her husband, a well-known and universally respected farmer, having died some years previously, found that she could make an acceptable addition to her income . . . by providing cyclists with tea and light refreshments . . .

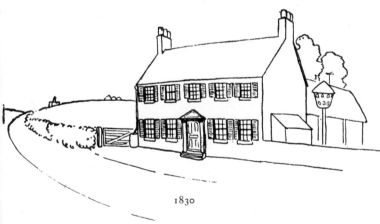

1830

numerous opportunities for comfortable sight-seeing to the present-day visitor to town. At the height of the season as many as fifty or sixty of these luxury coaches leave daily from the square opposite the town hall and almost as many bring visitors into the town from London and various neighbouring resorts . . .

Many of the thousands who, during the summer, motor down to Pelvis Bay by way of the new Flushbrook by-pass, must be familiar with the castellated tower of the 'Hearts Are Trumps'

1890

With the coming of the internal combustion engine
early in the present century her profits from this
source rapidly increased . . .

During the war, gallantly choosing as her motto
'Business as Usual', she drove a thriving trade with the
numerous lorry-drivers and others who were
continually passing on the way to the coast . . . in 1925,
when the old road was widened, straightened and
generally improved, it was decided to expand on a
large scale. With the aid of a local firm, Elizabethan
Enterprises Ltd, the old house was entirely recon-
structed in the Tudor style, seven lock-ups

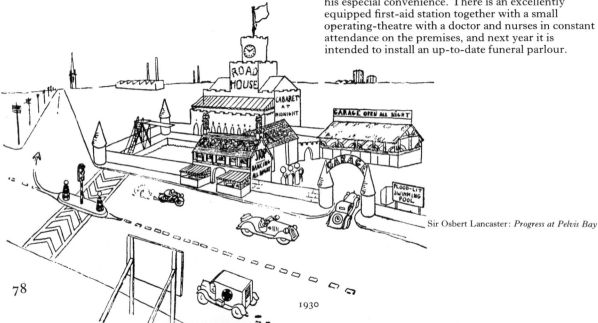

1925

were built, and, with considerable difficulty, a licence
obtained. Within a few months the 'Ace of Hearts', as
it was now called, was filled to capacity every week-end
during the summer, and even in winter did a
flourishing trade.

The next few years were ones of increasing
prosperity, and when, in 1930, the new Flushbrook
by-pass was opened, the vastly increased volume of
traffic found ample accommodation in the palatial new
premises of the 'Hearts Are Trumps' roadhouse. . . .
The garage had been increased in size and could now
accommodate over thirty cars at a time and ten new
petrol pumps had been installed. The Olde Englishe
Grille and the Restaurant Fleurie catered for all
tastes and supplied every species of fresh farm and

dairy produce straight from the Argentine, expertly
prepared by a large staff of skilled chefs. The American
Bar provided light refreshment for those who could
tarry long, and finally in the beautiful new dance hall,
with its modernistic sofas, Lalique panels and
cleverly concealed lighting, Ed Sugarprong and his
Twenty-Seven White-Hot Tubthumpers provided
the hottest jazz to be heard between Hammersmith
Broadway and Pelvis Bay. Last year the Pompeian
Swimming Pool, complete with artificial waves and
floodlit every night from seven till two, was opened
with a pretty ceremony in which forty of the loveliest
bathing belles in Britain took part.

The fastidious motorist will find at this
establishment that everything has been arranged for
his especial convenience. There is an excellently
equipped first-aid station together with a small
operating-theatre with a doctor and nurses in constant
attendance on the premises, and next year it is
intended to install an up-to-date funeral parlour.

Sir Osbert Lancaster: *Progress at Pelvis Bay*

1930

'Same as the one I drove in the Monte Carlo Rally.'

# Is This Your Car?

## IS THIS YOUR CAR?

The ubiquity of the motor car has given it a
power over our lives second only to that of
the H-bomb. The livelihood of millions of
people depend literally on the use or
possession of a motor vehicle of some sort.
For millions of others the deprivation of a
car would be a hardship hardly less acute.
A solemn thought. How, then, can we laugh
at a phenomenon so grave, so pregnant
with possible consequences of disaster? The
answer to that involves complex
psychological reasoning and this is not the
place for it. Isn't it enough that we are able
to laugh at the motorist and his car?

'Please fix my horn. My brakes don't work.'

*Dear Sir,*
    *Might I avail myself of your Readers' Letters column to publicly express my appreciation of this truly wonderful small car? I drive it flat out in all gears day in day out, frequently out-performing much bigger machinery, and I have nothing but praise for the very convenient engine exchange service. Mine was one of the very first models to be produced, and I can't wait for them to produce a Sports version. In nearly 12,000 miles I have put in no oil at all and have used only three engines. Marvellous.*

Red Daniells: *Drivers Wild*

'But you said you just wanted to get rid of the *car*!'

*Beneath this slab,*
*John Brown is stowed.*
*He watched the ads,*
*And not the road.*

Ogden Nash: *Good Intentions*

'Looks like a leak.'

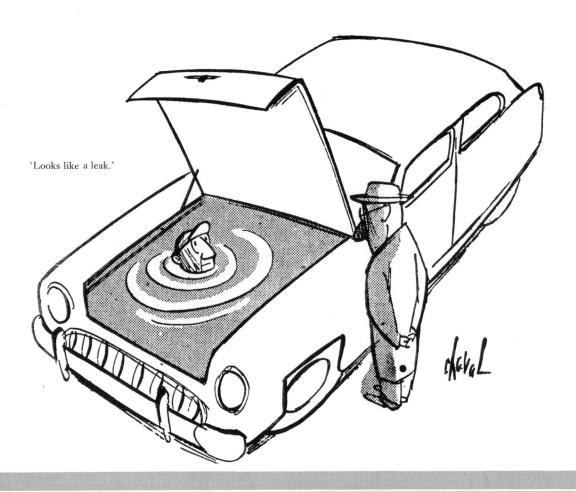

'Let's try the back roads – couldn't be slower.'

'Stephen usually opens the bonnet when something goes wrong.'

# Brockbank

'Darling, I can't afford to go on meeting you like this much longer.'

'Or look at it this way, sir –
buy a foreign car and you release
a British Leyland car for export.'

'Hold it, sir! That's only the *suggested* price!'

93

## Jonah (Basher) Swift

*President*
*The Association of By-pass Racing Motorists*

A man of strong (and many) convictions, he
was the outright winner of the Pile-up
Competition of 1964 and has been runner up
on a number of occasions.

In the study of his home at Crumpsall
are souvenirs of many of the incidents in
which he has been involved and others of
these are recorded on his driving licence.

At an early age he was barred from the
dodge-'em cars at the local Mop Fair and
took to the road as soon as he was able to
reach the pedals of a car. He has left his
mark in many places, for, as he says, 'It's
only on the road that a man can show his
real character.'

George Haines: *How to be a Motorist and Stay Happy*

'This car has double-dynamic suspension recoil. You know, springs.'

'Sorry, mate, usually those foreign cars are so reliable.'

'By jove, Sir, they don't make them like this any more!'

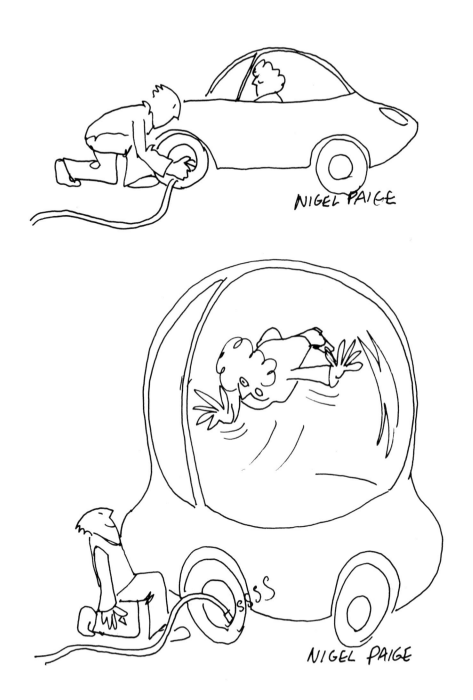

NIGEL PAIGE

NIGEL PAIGE

# Thelwell

'Don't panic, Cynthia, it's gravy.'

'A yellow plastic box marked "Sugar".'

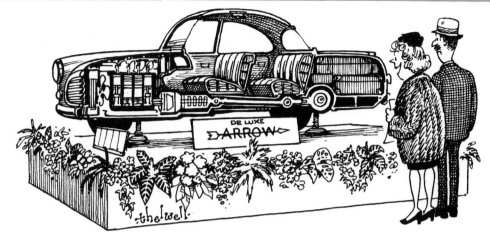

'Look at the depth of that carpet!'

OPTIONAL EXTRAS

Family Planning Clinic ahead

Beware of tyre slashers

Caution! Umbrella factory on left

The driver in front is drunk

Free bra with every four gallons

Beware of low flying motor cycles

Dumping of cars prohibited

Your left eye is stronger than your right

Good morning, sir. Is this your vehicle? Did you cause
it to be parked in this position for the past hour and
forty-seven minutes? You do realize that this is a
restricted area and that your vehicle constitutes an
obstruction? Of course, in the interests of better
police/public relationship I'll try to answer any
questions I can pertaining to the matter. Well, now,
the reason I'm not out catching murderers is that I'm
not on murderer-catching duty. I'm on traffic control
and you, sir, are traffic. What make of car is this?
Really? I don't think I've ever come across one before.
I hear they're very good. Bit pricey, though. As much
as that? Very nice for them that can afford it. Me, I
have to make do with the old push-bike. Mind you,
don't think I don't sympathize with you big car
owners. You'll never find anywhere legal to park a
thing this size and with all the paying out you do these
days I've no doubt you feel entitled to a bit of road to
put your car on. Honestly, I think you'd do very well
to keep your temper in these trying times. So I won't
add to your problems by wasting your time hanging
about here. If I could just see your licence and current
certificate of insurance and I must caution you . . .

Red Daniells: *Drivers Wildest*

'On a point of order, sir,
may I, with respect, interrupt
Parliamentary Question Time?'

DAVID LANGDON

NIGEL PAIGE

André François

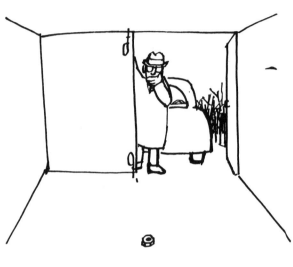

NIGEL PAIGE

'Once more round the block, O loved ones. We've got to use the damn stuff up somehow.'

# CARtoons by Robb

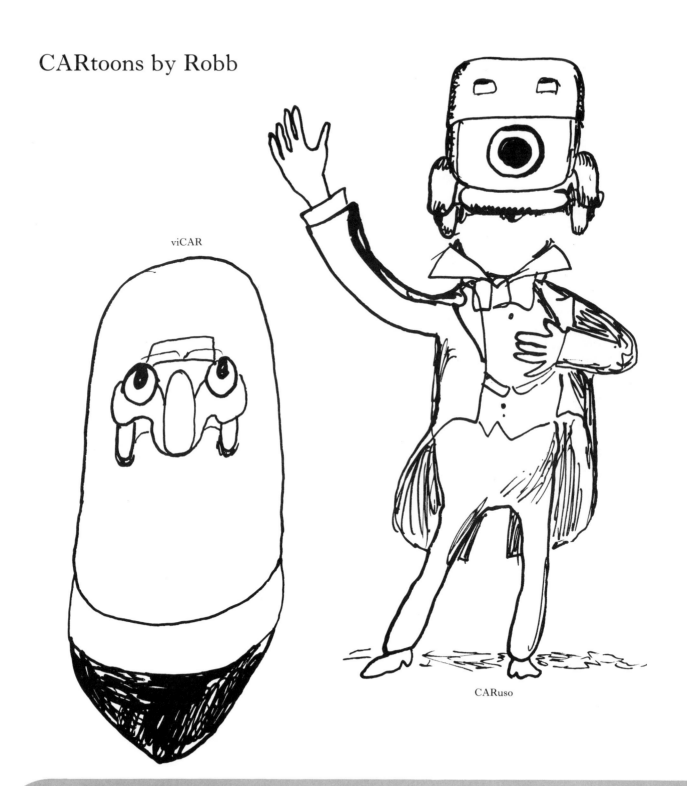

viCAR

CARuso

CARlsbad

CARdinal

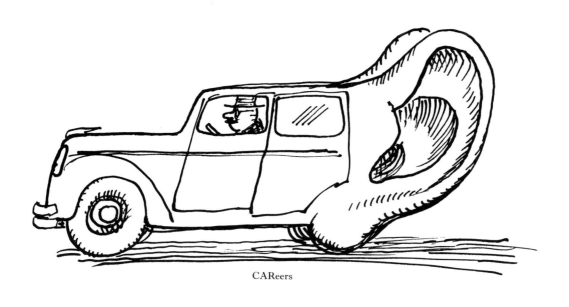

CAReers

CARthusian

CARdigan

We come up every year to have a look at the lights.
There's always something going on to have a look at.
Regent Street at Christmas, Blackpool in the autumn –
we always go and have a look. When we first used to go
on these outings I kept running into the back of
people, but after a bit I learnt to drive very slowly so as
to be able to stop. It's not so bad now as it used to be,
though, because what with the jams wherever there's
something to see you get a good chance to peer about
without having to keep moving. We used to have a car
with a sunshine roof and that was perfect for the
illuminations, but I still kept hitting things. I broke
my nose at the Southend fireworks and the windscreen
at the Son et Lumière. We always attend the Old
Crocks Race – very comical. We sometimes have a bit
of a race with them ourselves. Do you remember that
one that went clean off the road at Purley? I did that.
Accidentally, of course, but we had to laugh. I pulled
up short in front of him so's we could have a better
look and I reckon his brakes weren't up to much.
Still, where would all these be without our support?

Red Daniells: *More Wild Drivers*

'Me too. When they upped
the season tickets
I thought, Right,
there are other means
of transport.'

'A qualified Ministry of Transport examiner and you can't SWIM?'

Red Daniells

## SIGNS OF *THE TIMES*

Readers of *The Times* seem to be gifted with serendipity. After the publication of one or two unusual road signs, strange ambiguities spotted by observant readers of the paper were showered upon the editor, most of them products of the municipal mind, which moves in a mysterious way its blunders to perform.

'Ho, ho, ho – someone's travel allowance gone for a burton.'

'They're a waste of money – I've had just as
many accidents since I had them fitted.'

'Good heavens! You mean that nobody thought to bring a pair of scissors!'

# Ronald Searle

Düsseldorf

Ronald Searle, the leading British humorous artist of the post-war era, has for some years lived and worked in Paris, to the loss of the British press and the regret of his innumerable British admirers. Though his work is best known for its acute characterisation of individuals, he can turn his pen with equal facility to any subject and manages to invest the motor car with the same sort of scatty authenticity that he imparts to the human race.

Wolfsburg

Texas

California

'You're my first!'

'What double yellow line?'

'Illegally parking on cliff edge . . .
Being in charge of a vehicle with faulty brakes . . .!'

'And what makes you think I've been here *over* half an hour?'

# THE GAMBOLS . . . . .

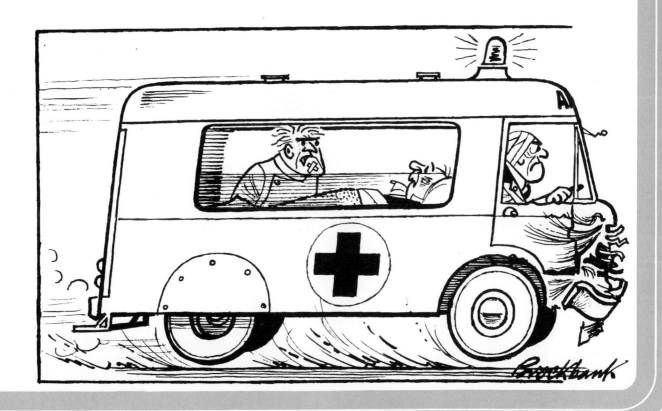

'Nothing wrong, thank you, officer –
it's just that I'm a terribly slow reader.'

'Strange . . . what does the atlas say?'

▶

# Being Sure of Shell

## BEING SURE OF SHELL

There are certain types of big business that seem to fight shy of introducing humour into their advertising, as though it might be thought an affront to their dignity. Shell is not one of those austere combines.

In the late twenties, the advertising of Shell-Mex, as it then was, took on a new lease of life under the inspired aegis of Jack Beddington, director of the firm's publicity and a man of dynamic and imaginative intelligence, which in the timorous, costive world of advertising is a rare thing to find. Around him Jack Beddington gathered an assembly of artists and wits from whom there came some of the most notable ideas that have ever been seen in British advertising. Among those who contributed to Shell's various schemes were Edward Ardizzone, Edward Bawden, John Betjeman (now Sir John), Barnett Freedman, E. McKnight Kauffer, Peter Quennell, Rex Whistler and many others, including John Reynolds, the artist who drew a figure that was to become familiar throughout Britain, Shell's double-headed workingman uttering the famous slogan, 'That's Shell – that was!'

At an exhibition of Shell advertising held not long before the Second World War, Robert Byron, writing in the catalogue, remarked, 'We are indebted to Shell for the dual pleasure of good art and good nonsense, sources of encouragement and laughter. . . .' The selection of Shell advertisements that follows shows that the gratitude expressed by Robert Byron was not misplaced.

"GRAVITY-FED."

*For Super Quality ask for "SHELL"*
*AVIATION MOTOR SPIRIT*

"Emily! I presume this is due to the quick-starting of 'Shell'!"

This nobleman is wondering
what he can be sure of in these days—

but his Lady has no doubts

She is Sure of Shell

–The Admiral was understood to reply, 'To Shell!'

REX WHISTLER

When the Midshipman asked where he should proceed to–

Some phrases seldom ring true

"pleased to meet you"

but

YOU CAN BE
SURE OF SHELL

Some phrases seldom ring true

"You can put your shirt on it"

but

YOU CAN BE
SURE OF SHELL

*You can't pick holes
In a Rolls
It would almost be silly
For SHELL to gild the lily*

*You go very fast very gently
In a Bentley.
With Shell you'll go faster,
gentlier,
In fact — Bentlier.*

# Times change - - - so does SHELL

"We must move with the times, you know . . ." How often said, and how seldom acted upon! For over thirty years Shell has moved with the times, constantly adapting itself to the ever more exacting demands of motor engines. Shell progresses by steady evolution, and can justly claim to be the petrol of the past, the present, and the future.

Dear Santa

Is that Harridges?

Brian Robb

# *Times Change,* so does SHELL

It took an age to write a long scrawly letter to Santa! And even then he might bring the wrong present. Now it's all done in a trice on the telephone.

Getting Christmas presents is an altogether quicker affair to-day: so is getting about. The development of motor cars and motor engines to their present standard of efficiency has been a gradual one. As each small improvement has been made, so Shell too has changed to meet the new demands made upon it. Because it never stands still, Shell has maintained and will always maintain its reputation for giving the best performance.

# Shell Guide to the Affluent Society

No. 2 The Personalized Car

STRATFORD SPECIAL

N.U.T.

L.R.C.D.S.

SHOW BIZ

F.R.P.S.

HIGH REVS

SHELLIST

Hillman Husky

Jaguar

Triumph Spitfire

Riley Elf

Morris Oxford

Ρώλλς Ροῖς

## Plate VI
### The Multi-Headed Badge Bar

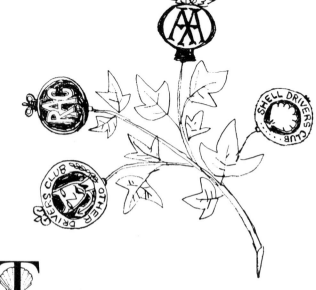

Tʜɪs luxuriant growth can sprout a dozen blooms from one chromium stem. Look out for:

**AA**   Yellow flower. Often cultivated at short notice at the top of Porlock Hill.

**RAC**   Blue flower. The indoor town plant is rather rarer than the common rambler.

**ODC**   Other Drivers' Club. A rare specie who actually believe they drive no better than the next man.

**SDC**   Shell Drivers' Club. Universally popular. No badge, but club premises blossom every few miles all over Europe.

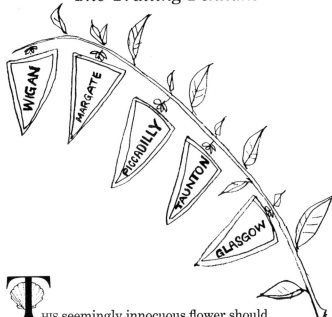

# THE SHELL BOOK OF NATURAL MOTORING

## Plate VII

### *The Trailing Pennant*

**T**HIS seemingly innocuous flower should
not be allowed to run riot. Generally planted
at irregular intervals on safety glass or
trained up wireless aerials. Thin out, if visibility
is impaired. The more commonplace blooms
cover virtually the whole British Isles.
One reader writes: *Why no Shell pennant?*
Because, of course, everybody goes to Shell.

Aesop Shell

The winner of the race
   was easy to foretell.
The hare had all the pace–
   But the tortoise had the Shell

LLANFAIRPWLLGWYNGYLLGOGERYCHWYRNDROBWLL-LLANTYSILIOGOGOGOCH

BUT **SHELL** *LLASTS LLONGEST*

EDWARDES *SQUARE* — BUT

**SHELL'S** *a good all round petrol*

HENLEY-on-THAMES

BUT

SHELL

ON THE ROAD

GERRARD'S *CROSS*

BUT **SHELL**'S *PLEASING*

## *Chorlton-cum-Hardy*

## *Winter Shell come Monday*

# TENNIS AT WIMBLEDON

Why are all eyes on Wimbledon ? Watching
DIFFERENCES, to be sure !  Differences ?
Yes, the vital little differences that make
one player supreme amongst many good
ones just as the DIFFERENCE of Shell
from other petrols makes it the acknowledged champion of the road

# THE BOAT RACE

Everyone loves this typically English event in which pluck and preparation alone give that margin of difference that wins. It is like the difference of Shell petrol, which is balanced and re-balanced from ingredients tested and re-tested until it attains a perfection that wins in every test where sheer efficiency counts

# Acknowledgments

9 Published in France in 1818 (by courtesy of the 'Mansell Collection')

10 Engraving by Henry Alken 1828 (by courtesy of the 'Mansell Collection')

11 Engraving by Henry Alken, *The Picture Magazine*, 1829 (by courtesy of the 'Mansell Collection')

12 George Cruikshank, 1829 (by courtesy of the 'Mansell Collection')

13 *above* W. Ralston from 'The Story of an Auto-Motor Car' No. 2, 1896 (by courtesy of the Radio Times Hulton Picture Library)

13 *below* Ralph Cleaver, 1899 (by courtesy of the 'Mansell Collection')

14 Two humorous postcards (by courtesy of The National Motor Museum)

17 Signed G.D.D., *Punch* 1897 (by courtesy of the Mary Evans Picture Library)

18, 19 Four postcards (by courtesy of The National Motor Museum)

20 B. Rabier, *Le Rire* 1899 (by courtesy of the Mary Evans Picture Library)

21 A. Robida, *Nature* 1895 (by courtesy of the Mary Evans Picture Library)

22 *above* C. Harrison, *Punch* 1901 (by courtesy of the Mary Evans Picture Library)

22 *below* Georges Meunier, *Le Rire* 1900 (by courtesy of the Mary Evans Picture Library)

23 Caran d'Ache, 'Album des Lundis', Paris

24 *above* Lucien Métivet (by courtesy of the Mary Evans Picture Library)

24 *below* Michelin Tyre Co. Ltd

25 A. Robida, *Nature* 1903 (by courtesy of the Mary Evans Picture Library)

26 H. C. Jallano, *Punch* 1900 (by courtesy of the Mary Evans Picture Library)

27 Caran d'Ache, 'Gros et Detail', Paris

28 Postcard signed Tom B. (by courtesy of The National Motor Museum)

29 L. Sabattier, 1905 (by courtesy of the 'Mansell Collection')

30 René Bull, *The Sketch* 1906 (by courtesy of the 'Mansell Collection')

31, 32, 33 Signed A.S.B., *Punch* 1906 (by courtesy of the 'Mansell Collection')

34 Poem, Harry Graham, 'Most Ruthless Rhymes for Heartless Homes', Edward Arnold (Publishers) Ltd, 1974

34 Signed G.C.H. 'Most Ruthless Rhymes' by Harry Graham, Edward Arnold (Publishers) Ltd, 1974

35 René Bull, *Punch* 1906 (by courtesy of the 'Mansell Collection')

36 Villemot, *Le Rire* 1906 (by courtesy of the Mary Evans Picture Library)

37 L. Raven Hill, *Punch* 1901 (by courtesy of the Mary Evans Picture Library)

38 L. Raven Hill, *Punch* 1901 (by courtesy of the Mary Evans Picture Library)

39 *Punch* 1914 (by courtesy of the Mary Evans Picture Library)

40 Lawson Wood, *The Sketch* 1906 (by courtesy of the 'Mansell Collection')

43–52 H. M. Bateman, 'A Book of Drawings', Methuen, 1921 (the executors of the artist)

53–4 Text, Maurice Wiggin, 'In Spite of the Price of Hay', Phoenix House, 1956

54 John Hassell, from the Mary Evans Picture Library (the Ford Motor Co. Ltd)

55 Poem, Harry Graham, 'Most Ruthless Rhymes', Edward Arnold (Publishers) Ltd, 1974

55 Ridgewell, 'Most Ruthless Rhymes', Edward Arnold (Publishers) Ltd, 1974

56 Michelin Tyre Co. Ltd

57 *Motor Commerce*, 1926 (by courtesy of the Automobile Association)

58 Poem, H. S. Mackintosh, 'Ballades and other Verses', Rupert Hart-Davis, 1952

59 W. Heath Robinson (the executors of the artist)

60 W. Heath Robinson, 'Motor Mania' published by *The Motor Owner* (the executors of the artist)

61, 62 W. Heath Robinson, 1938 (the executors of the artist)

63 Text, Sir Max Beerbohm, 'Mainly on the Air', William Heinemann, 1946

64 Poem, Harry Graham, 'Most Ruthless Rhymes', Edward Arnold (Publishers) Ltd, 1974

64 Ridgewell, 'Most Ruthless Rhymes' by Harry Graham, Edward Arnold (Publishers) Ltd, 1974

65–6 Text, Donald McCullough, 'You have been Warned', Methuen and Co. Ltd, 1935

65–67 Fougasse, 'You have been Warned' by Fougasse and McCullough, Methuen, 1935 (Associated Book Publishers Ltd)

68 Arthur Watts, *Punch* 1925 (by courtesy of the 'Mansell Collection')

69, 70 Frank Reynolds, '*Punch* Pictures', Cassell, 1922

71 Frank Reynolds, *Punch* 1920 (by courtesy of the 'Mansell Collection')

72 Poems, Sir John Betjeman, 'Summoned by Bells', 1960 and 'Continual Dew', 1937, John Murray (Publishers) Ltd

72 W. Heath Robinson, 'Motor Mania', published by *The Motor Owner* (the executors of the artist)

73 Peter Arno, 'Peter Arno's Parade', John Lane the Bodley Head

74, 75 David Low, *Evening Standard* 1936 (by

## List of Cartoonists

## List of Writers